F
TOZ
YOUR
CULTURE

DAHC SLOKIN

HOW BUSINESS,

RELIGION,

ATHLETES,

AND HUMANITY

HAVE IT ALL WRONG

F Your Culture

©2021 Chad Nichols

edited by "THE" Don Pavey

print ISBN: 978-1-09839-153-9
ebook ISBN: 978-1-09839-154-6

CONTENTS

INTRODUCTION

WARNING! IF YOU ARE SOME PANTYWAIST HUMAN THAT GETS OFFENDED BY ANYTHING AND EVERYTHING, SOME SNOWFLAKE THAT STILL LIVES IN MOMMY'S BASEMENT, OR JUST AN ASSCLOWN THAT DOESN'T BELIEVE IN FACTS.... THEN THIS BOOK IS GOING TO SEND YOU INTO A FULL-BLOWN SEIZURE.................FOR SURE!!!!

*************Caution Heavy Language*************

Let me introduce myself. I'm the kid that grew up in a blue-collar town south of Atlanta, Georgia. A town called Riverdale where a bunch of 1980's bad ass guys and gals lived our lives to the fullest, and cared for each other like we were family (GO RAIDERS).

I grew up with parents that CARED about what I made of myself and introduced me to a work ethic that is NO LONGER EXISTENT IN THIS COUNTRY (predominantly in the youth of today and when I say "youth,"

35 years of age and below). I am THAT guy who worked tirelessly day after day, hour after grueling hour, never taking a vacation. The guy that always went above and beyond, never calling in sick. The guy that answered his phone for customers twenty four hours a day even on holidays. And the guy that never quit...............................
UNTIL NOW!!!!

Quitter? Never in my wildest dreams did I ever think that word would come out of my mouth. I was raised to "never quit" no matter how bad it got for me. I was raised to get through it, and I always did. This word is especially important in this book and will be brought up several times. I will explain to you each detail of why the word "QUITTER" makes me smile now.

After 35 years of working with the highest loyalty, drive, and ethic, I will detail what I have learned and how I have seen the decline in religion, media, athletes, business and humanity.

I am not a so-called "expert" because no one really is. The media just likes to tout college degrees and people that have knowledge in one field over another that fit their agenda, meanwhile contradicting "experts" get silenced.

I do, however, believe I have an ancient mystical thought process NOT OFTEN SEEN ON EARTH.......
called "COMMON SENSE." I know, I know.... you are

calling bullshit on this one. You know as well as I do that "common sense" is a hoax these days, and only mentioned in the DEAD SEA SCROLLS!!!! That last statement might as well be true due to a LACK of "common sense" in the world today.

I hope you enjoy my passion and whether you believe what I say or not, I'm going to say what most of you want to say in public, but are just too scared to for fear of reprisal and losing the "almighty dollar" you have sold your soul for. You might offend someone, right? FUCK IT!!!!

ENTER AT YOUR OWN RISK!!!!!!!!

RELIGION

OHHHHHHHH I AM ABOUT TO MAKE YOU sprinkle HOLY WATER all over your house after reading this one. Get over yourself and your belief for just a moment and truly listen to what I am saying. I may be right, and I may be off my rocker, but what I am about to write is something I have observed over the years. I QUESTION THE INTENTIONS OF CHRISTIANS (or shall I say "hypochristians").

IS YOUR BLOOD PRESSURE UP YET? ....
GOOD! LET'S GET INTO THIS.

This will probably be the shortest chapter of this book. Yet, who knows because I have just begun, and know not what is going to come to mind while putting it down on paper.

I was raised in one specific religion as a kid. We were taught that OUR religion was the "right" one. Friends of mine that were raised in other religions were taught the same, that their religion was the "right" one. So, over the years between the people I met and different religions I learned of, I've grown to understand that each person truly believes in their religion and KNOWS, beyond a shadow of a doubt, that "their" religion is "the one." WELL, WHICH ONE IS IT?

How do we know which religion is right or wrong? I suppose religions that want to kill you for not subscribing to their specific ideology might be seen as "wrong", but don't take my word for it, who am I to love life? If someone's religion is not the same as yours, are THEY going to hell or just not going as "high in heaven" as you are, since yours is the right one? Or are we even going to heaven? We are being pretty presumptuous thinking that our religion (that is obviously superior to everyone else's religion) is going to bring us to heaven's gates……. RIGHT?

Listen, I am not dogging on ANY specific religion so let's get that straight right now (go take your blood pressure medicine before you stroke out on me…. I want you to finish this book, you bought it, so get your money's worth).

It is my belief that most of us who believe in a higher power or something similar, are on the same page. Each religion has its "do and do not" rules. I believe that the Lord Jesus Christ is my savior. Some do not, and that is ok.

There are a ton that believe the same as I do, with similar beliefs under a different name, and those are the ones I am talking to. Some religions believe in saints while some believe in different levels of heaven. Some religions believe that you can be "born again" and be forgiven of all your sins, even if you commit them again and again.

I do believe that we are forgiven, and God is a very forgiving God, but understand there is a limit to how many times he will forgive the same sin without punishment (MY opinion of course).

("Hey little Johnny, I see you committed the same sin for the 240th time.....you are forgiven!! ~God") Mmmmmmmmmmmmmmmm......better hope so!!!

I do not believe in certain ideals that some religions teach. This viewpoint comes from not only applying the ideals I was personally raised to believe, but from applying "common sense" to determine how far-fetched and political a religious rule or decision might be. HELL, I don't even believe in some of the "ideals" my own religion teaches.

For the most part, Religious Culture as a whole is very similar. There is a thought process to what each religion believes, and each one has a following. Followers are more often than not, people that look at different religions and decide on what fits "THEM" best. Not necessarily what "is" best, but how much effort that individual is willing to give to fulfill "everlasting life" (if there is such a thing, right?) Some people today are raised in one religion, and because they were "forced" by their parents to go to church every Sunday, they rebel and choose to leave that religion for another, or decide to just call themselves "spiritual." I see nothing wrong with this at all, but again it goes back to an individual's effort and how strong their belief is in their faith, or in my opinion, how prevalent their laziness is. Some people use the excuse "I'm spiritual" just so they don't have to go to church and get their lazy ass out of bed after partying all night.... *c'mon.... we know who you are!!*

I have watched the evolution of my religion as I grew in age and mind. I have questioned many things that I was taught to be true as a kid and have thought otherwise since. For instance, I now question whether certain rules in my religion are "man-made." Do they align with the actual teachings of Christ? As we get older and begin to realize that nothing is perfect in life, not even religion, we may start to question it. Why were we taught a certain way to believe? (Hold that thought, I will come back to it.)

Enter the word "Culture." It is our nature to live under a certain culture as humans. We find what we like and adapt ourselves to "that culture" and live under those guidelines we have made for ourselves, and that of which our "culture" has drawn out for us. In religion, each one has a culture that believes their thought process and God is the right one, even though each "God" is the same one for the most part. We are taught that we cannot listen to other religions or their belief systems, unless they believe what we believe to be right.............does that make sense? (Keep reading, it gets better.)

THIS THOUGHT PROCESS is where I became a "QUITTER." With all the knowledge I have gathered over the years, I do love my religion and I AM NOT quitting my faith. But please understand that I will question the humans at the highest level of this faith, and hold them accountable for decisions made. So, what have I QUIT? Good question. I quit believing that my religion was better than all the others, and I do not believe the others are better than mine. I quit thinking that if you were not "my religion" that your faith was wrong. Christianity AS A WHOLE has become "hypochristianity." We will sit in the pew on Sunday and as soon as we are pulling out of the parking lot, cuss the person that was sitting next to you for pulling out in front of you, trying to LEAVE church!!!

(Hell, you fuckers can't even get out of the parking lot without saying the Lord's name in vain)

We will have Sunday dinners with our families and then a few days later we talk behind each other's backs (bless their hearts)!!!!! WHAT IS GOING ON PEOPLE????

How is it that we can give our lives to God and then curse or slander his very creation with a person we do not agree with? Hell, I find myself doing it too. Is it human nature to do this? Is it the way of mankind to be productive toward one goal, yet counterproductive toward the same?

I QUIT!!!!! I believe God is a very forgiving God. I believe all religions have right and wrong in them. I believe that we have fallen into a culture of belief that the one religion we practice, or in some cases don't practice, is the only one. WRONG!!!!

There is an attack on CHRISTIANITY taking place all over the world. If we do not start branching out to help other religions when they are attacked, we will all go down one by one. The largest will fall first. When that one falls, Katy bar the doors because the war will be in full play. We have lulled ourselves to sleep in the belief that praying alone with "our" religion will be "good enough." GUESS WHAT…………….. WE ARE WRONG!!!!! God gave his archangels weapons KNOWING prayer alone could not defeat evil…...stew on that one for a while.

CHRISTIANITY is being attacked. Yet we sit back and watch when an outside religion is attacked, and form a barrier around our own. We built this country on "FREEDOM OF RELIGION." That NO GOVERNMENT can tell us how and when we can practice our chosen faith. That NO

GOVERNMENT can force us to practice one faith and not another. WE FOUGHT FOR THIS AND WON. Yet we take it for granted and hunker down, hoping that they won't come for us. Regardless of which religion is attacked, IF WE DON'T FIGHT FOR RELIGIOUS FREEDOM WE......WILL.... LOSE!!!!! If we don't get over our "culture", and continue to think that we must refuse to offer a helping hand or voice to uplift someone because of an opposing ideology ..........WE.......WILL........LOSE!!!!!

For too long we have been brainwashed into thinking that we cannot help a competing religion. REALLY?? SINCE WHEN WAS THIS A COMPETITION??? There are no ribbons for first place. The reward is GETTING there.

For example, my Mother once asked a member of a different religion, "if we were to run out of food and needed help would you be able to help feed our family with your food supply?" The member stated, "NO, we are not allowed to help another religion." WHAAAAAAAAAAT????? HOW ABOUT HELPING HUMANITY, or is that the wrong religion too!!? This is a true story!!!!

What Bible or document did you read that said, "THE LORD ONLY HELPS THOSE THAT WERE OF HIS KIND?" THIS GUY WALKED WITH LEPERS for "Christ's" sake!!!!!! In what world do you think that the God of all Gods would only choose one race, religion, sex, country, planet, or HUMAN? We have a gift, and that gift was instilled in us by Jesus Christ.

Some do not believe in religion at all. That is ok, but understand that "Freedom of Religion" protects those that do not believe as well. How is that, you might ask?? If those that do not believe think that they are given a pass and do not have to fight for freedom of religion...........think again. As one religion falls due to government regulations or rules or whatever they come up with, your freedom of non-religion is on the chopping block too. Control is what those in power want. COMPLETE CONTROL, so that everyone thinks the same and there is no resistance. (For example, if the powers that be want everyone worshipping the cabbage head, you fuckers that don't believe at all, will now be worshipping the cabbage head................ GET IT?)

So, "F YOUR CULTURE" of not helping everyone. Start understanding that politics are very prevalent in religion, and they use it against you every day without you even knowing it. You are in a brainwashing battle, and you don't even know that you are in the arena of war!!! OPEN YOUR EYES to your freedoms being taken away. Quitting this culture made me realize how much God wants us to understand that everyone matters, and if we do not fight to keep what we have by helping ALL religions when attacked, then what kind of "Christian" are we ultimately? Let me answer that with "hypochristian." The shepherds need to guide their flock, but as they do they also need to speak to other shepherds and combine forces for protection. Christianity cannot fail!!! If you do not Defend Heaven on Earth, you will not have a chance to Defend Heaven!!! GET IT?

(P.S. to show you this chapter rings true. I had a conservative "Christian" publishing company turn down the publishing of this book because of the title of it……….. HYPOCHRISTIANS!!!!)

IS YOUR BLOOD BOILING YET? Are you cussing me out? If not…………keep reading. I will get you there soon enough. You are either going to hate that you bought this book or sit back at the end of it and say, "this crazy son of a bitch has something here." Need a potty break? Hurry up, I have way more to say.

SPORTS

WHAAAAAAAAAAAAAT IN THEEEEE FUCK HAVE WE DONE TO SPORTS????? BETTER YET, the real question is "What have we let sports do to us?"

I grew up in a baseball family. My family has over 100 combined years of service in professional baseball. I lived and breathed baseball during each season. I would go to the ballpark with my grandfather during spring training. I would watch how he guided his players and his coaches.

We would bring home broken bats from the spring training games and saw them in half for firewood. (I was a kid. I was not worried about Hall of Fame memorabilia. I wanted to use power tools) I...LOVED...BASEBALL!!!

As I grew up, I would open the paper and check the game stats from the previous day. I would see how my uncle played and check his stats for the day. I would look to see how my grandfather's (he was a GM/VP of many teams) team fared in their games from the day prior. It used to be fun to watch KNOWING that you were watching a game that these guys loved to play. (I do not know if you noticed what I called it, but I'll say it again, "watching a GAME!!")

The competition was fierce, and the camaraderie was amazing, or so it seemed to me at the time. I remember going down to the club house when my uncle's team was in town. He would leave us tickets at will call. As a small child I met "THE" Mr. Wrigley on his private jet. I ate breakfast with Pete Rose and Tommy Lasorda at a baseball convention. I looooooooooooved baseball. My Grandfather was best friends with Ted Williams for God's sake. I met more baseball players through my family or through work than I can remember, and NEVER ONCE asked for an autograph!!!! I LOVED THE GAME!!!!

I remember watching football with my Dad on Sundays and Mondays, back when you could hit someone in football and not have a flag thrown. Watching basketball, I remember witnessing Larry Bird shoot 3 pointers alllllllllllllllllllllll dayyyyyyyyyyy loooooooooooong and Kareem Abdul-Jabbar sky hooking like the ball was meant to be shot that way. I was always amazed at how accurate they were. I would watch Magic Johnson glide up the court like he was on skates. Speaking of "gliding", Clyde "the Glide" Drexler was an outstanding basketball player with some sick-ass dunks. HELL, I remember when you got called for traveling if you took more than two steps, and GROWN MEN didn't fall to the floor like they just got their ass kicked while barely being touched by the opponent. THAT WAS SPORTS!!!!! THOSE WERE MEN PLAYING BACK THEN. Now……. we have snowflakes in every sport that get butt hurt at everything. But whose fault is it? (I will answer that soon)

To show you how old I am, I remember when Team USA, no matter the sport, showed respect to their country and honored the flag for the freedom it represents. Being proud of our country was never questioned. No matter what race you were, your pride in the USA was absolute. The Olympics was a coveted event every two years. Our country was proud of athletes, and our athletes were proud of their country. Americans would have their radios on at work listening to every syllable from the commentators for every game. We would hurry home in hopes to see us win the gold. Now, the Athletes have wrecked this stage and the "Once great event," is almost a memory for most.

WHAT HAVE WE ALLOWED SPORTS TO DO TO US? I will tell you what they do to us. They control us. They have worked their way so deep into our "culture" of life that they can now say and do anything they want, KNOWING you will not do a damn thing about it.

We have allowed the gradual take over from owners that held a little respect for the game, to investment groups that want money, and are willing to allow the players to say and do anything they want AS LONG AS it doesn't hurt the bottom line. *(Remember what I just said about the bottom line....it comes up again)*

We used to have owners of teams that controlled the "nonsense" that came from the players. Although there are "some" players that are pretty damn smart, most athletes made it through school on their athletic ability, let's not fool ourselves. Listening to them speak at interviews proves that point. Athletes are there to PLAY...... THE....... GAME!!!!

They are not there to tell us their opinion on ANYTHING (unless it is about the game they JUST played). Play the damn game!!! We pay you to entertain us and do superhuman shit. THAT'S ALL!!! *(did you catch what I just said...."WE PAY"....not the owners pay)* I do not care what your dog's name is or who you are voting for. I do think you are an asshole if you beat your wife, but that is for the law to figure out. I do not care what drugs are in your system *(although I would like to see steroids and growth hormone legalized for professional athletes so they can recover faster and do more SUPERHUMAN SHIT!!!! My opinion, of course, but that is another book altogether).*

What I do care about is when I turn on the TV and watch the game I want to watch, that athletes realize IT ISN'T THEIR STAGE!!!!! This stage is the people's stage. The people that pay to watch you do your thing. The fans that buy your gear and wait for hours, in hopes that one of you arrogant bastards will sign their ball, card, or hat. We DON'T CARE if you do not like the National Anthem, stand anyway, you are in AMERICA. We do not care if you don't like cops (that is between you and the cops, and of course when your mansion gets broken into the first people you are going to call are, ... wait for it...................... COPS!!!!)

We want to see you and all the gifts God gave you to catch and throw a ball. We want to see the BAD ASS defensive ends crush the O'LINE and pulverize the quarterback for a loss. We want to see the outstretched arms of a receiver haul in an impossible grab, or a throw from center field to home plate that comes in as a strike and DOESN'T EVEN ONE HOP THE PLATE!!!!!! Is it too much to ask? (Keep reading!!!!)

We have idolized these athletes to a point that they actually believe they are important to society. Hell, one of them said, "I am too important to society to keep my mouth shut". NO.................. NO YOU ARE NOT!!!!! Who lied to you and told you that you were important or smart enough to do ANYTHING but play your sport?

Your paycheck does not equate to IQ level.....TRUST ME!!!! When your career is over and you want to venture out and try something new, then and ONLY THEN will we watch to see if you are any good at that shit. IT'S NOT YOUR STAGE!!!!

We have let our children watch these athletes bash each other, and our nation, and told them that it is ok.

"Hey, Johnny. It is ok that your favorite athlete hates America and cops, and maybe even everyone, so just keep watching him or her because their opinion matters" ....*IT DOESN'T!!!!*

You should be talking with "little Johnny" about how wrong it is, if you really care about your kids. Why do we keep letting the athlete control our hard-earned money?

We have allowed our kids to continually idolize HORRIBLE people by not saying a word about what comes from their mouths or actions. By being silent about what is written on their jerseys or taped on their helmets, we have told our kids that it is ok to disrespect this country by kneeling for your agenda instead of ACTUALLY BEING THANKFUL for the opportunity FREEDOM has given you. MAKES TOO MUCH SENSE, RIGHT?????

We have watched athletes profess "I'm a man of God" for their entire career, and then proceed to wear a felon's name on their helmet. Why? ONLY TO CEMENT their Hall of Fame bid from being jeopardized!!! These athletes do not care that their names are being bastardized, they just want to secure the money. We sit and watch as almost every arena of sports says that only one type of life matters, when as Christians, or at the very least....... HUMANS, we should be telling them that every life matters no matter what color you are. But we continue to buy their tickets.

Why do we allow "athletes" to do this? I'll tell you why. We idolize those on TV as important people, and we fail to realize that they are JUST HUMAN. They are better at "that sport" than us, and incredibly talented at that. We fail to do simple math and realize that although they may be good at sports, most of them SUCK at economics, a shit ton of them suck at HISTORY, and almost all of them suck at being HUMBLE!!!!! (Hence the prior statement about making it through school on their athletic ability and nothing else)

We fail to teach our kids that certain things that are uttered from their favorite athletes' mouths, are actually false. Most of these guys and gals are just throwing up what they heard on tv, read on the internet, or have been PAID TO SAY. There is no research done on 99% of their statements AT ALL. For example, when one athlete calls cops racist but has also stated he doesn't want any friends or anything to do with anyone that IS NOT his color...........ARE YOU KIDDING ME? This all comes from parents FAILING to be parents and having an actual place in their kid's life.

Other than coming home from work saying "hello" and the occasional video game that parents might play with their kids, what exactly are you doing to teach little Johnny right from wrong.........YOU ARE NOT TEACHING LITTLE JOHNNY SHIT AND THAT IS WHY YOUR KID HAS NOW JOINED ANTIFA!!!! He still has his face in a phone all day, his pants are sagging, his school grades suck, he has no respect for others, he can't even sign his damn name without it looking like hieroglyphics, and yet you are silent on all of this......GREAT JOB.......... DAD!!!! (Don't let me get off track here. Parenting, or lack of is yet another book to be written.)

We have lifted our sports and those that compete in them, and made them superior to us......WHY?

CULTURE....... that's why. We grew up this way. We watched and enjoyed famous people on TV as well as athletes that made us feel good and that we could be proud of. We watched UNKNOWING of who these people were in real life. Unknowing of their drug habit, wife-beating, racist views, and so on. We did not know AND WE DIDN'T CARE!!!! BUT THEN CAME THE INTERNET. Now we knew everything. We would hear about all the bad crap that these athletes did and there was no stone left unturned. We were in the thick of things, but it did not matter to us. We were so engrossed in our "CULTURE" of doing things that we could not stop, or better yet refused to stop watching it. This was "our team." This was the sport we grew up with on Sundays, and we never missed a game throughout the week because that is all we knew to do. Our "culture" did not allow our minds to escape it, so it was all overlooked. We overlooked it so much that we KEPT WATCHING even when "our team" knelt because they said our National Anthem was racist. Do we even know the story about how the National Anthem came about?

The Battle of Baltimore where the English were bombarding our fort. Francis Scott Key was imprisoned on an English ship watching this very battle. He could see our flag flying high. Cannon after cannon struck our fort and the English were relentless in the fight. Their very mission was to shoot the flag and make it fall. As Francis Scott Key watched through the night the Flag still stood. He could not believe it. "As the rockets' red glare gave proof through the night, that our flag was still there." In this battle what was unseen is that it was so important to keep that flag raised that the fort was piling casualties around the base of the flagpole, to keep the pole standing. Our men that FOUGHT for this FREEDOM that these athletes so easily dismiss were piled around OLD

GLORY to keep it standing. "FOR THE LAND OF THE FREE, AND THE HOME OF THE BRAVE." (Thank God we didn't have pro athletes back in the day. They would have thrown the flag of surrender just seeing a "picture" of the English ships coming in, much less getting attacked)

How many of you knew that little-known fact? I guarantee 99% of these athletes today have no clue what happened, and they certainly have NO CLUE what freedom means. (Hell, if you don't kneel you lose your "street cred" right? ASSCLOWNS!!!)

Why do you think that kids idolize athletes? Why did you as a child idolize an athlete or individual on tv? If you are around my age, "that is what we did." We learned it. We thought enough of our friends and family that we copied and grew to like what they liked. Or we wanted competition, so we decided to like the rival teams and players. We wanted to be "that" star athlete so much that we practiced hard to get there. We would play in the street and act like we were them. We even took on the names of our favorite players and wanted their number on our sports jerseys.

As you grew in the game and the game grew on you, certain players and teams became your favorite. Perhaps it was because they were a cool guy or girl and you liked their colors and helmets, or their badass play on the field?

Whatever it was, you grew in the game and the game became your culture. When the game was on, NOTHING was more important. If your team lost, you were in a bad mood all week until they had a chance to win again. Then on THAT day, they were forgiven, and it was on like Donkey Kong with you running your mouth to your friends about how "my team" is going to whoooooooooooooooop dat asssssssssssssssss!!!! RIGHT?

What does it take to get your attention? Why do we allow athletes from all sports to do as they please on a stage that is made for OUR ENTERTAINMENT? Instead of watching two teams compete, now every event is in jeopardy of becoming some kind of political statement, so that one of these assclowns can feel important. Every commercial we watch has some hidden agenda in it. (more on commercials in the "Business" chapter)

IT IS NOT THEIR STAGE!!!!! When are we going to realize that "we" control whether they do this or not?

As humans, we take the easy way around things. It is exceedingly rare that the road less traveled is gone down, because there is a reason it is less traveled. IT IS HARDER!!!! The road less traveled is meant for leaders and entrepreneurs. Most humans do not have the strength of mind, nor the discipline to take this road. Laziness is a word that comes to my mind.

These athletes were once those types of leaders as they came up through the system. The athletes that make it to pro status or what is called "The Show" have walked the road that many do not. They have busted their asses as small children working on their craft to make it to "the bigs." These athletes did not party in high school. They were focused on their dream in college and one day it all paid off for them when they were drafted into their sports "Pro Division." WE MADE IT!!!! WE DID IT!!!! All that hard work paid off and now we are getting paid to play our sport. A dream come true. Then they SCREW THE POOCH by opening their mouth and losing the very discipline that got them to "THE SHOW."

The first few years of a young athlete's career you see humility in them, and a willingness to learn their place. Their interviews go something like this,

> *"I am grateful to be here and have this opportunity to help my team. We are in a good spot, and we have so much talent here. I thank God for leading my way and I hope I can be a good ambassador to the sport."*

Then as they see a little success and get the "big contract" having shown their worth to the organization, they start getting cocky. You see the celebrations on the touchdown or goals getting a little more dramatic. The "bat flips" a little higher and watching the ball leave the park takes a little longer KNOWING the pitcher hates it, but they feel like getting beaned the next time at bat for some reason.

They find the TV camera and make sure they are being filmed. It no longer is about the team, but about "them" and "their" worth TO the team. Now their interviews sound something like this,

> *"It was a good game. I was happy with how I played tonight. With my talents I bring to the team we have a better chance of winning every night. I would have liked to have seen the ball thrown my way a little more because I was open and could have made some plays. We will just see what next week brings and how I feel about the tempo of the game."*

Obviously, that is an over exaggeration, but they go from humble "how can I help my team" to "Me, Me, Me", and this is true more times than not. Very rarely do we find an athlete that can remain focused on team efforts over their own as their career advances. Then you get the real sociopathic athletes that miraculously wake up one day and think they should have a say in who is drafted, and how the organization functions. Some go as far as telling you

how "society as a whole" should function................
JUST PLAY THE DAMN GAME!!!!!

Why does this happen? CULTURE, and the wrong kind. The owners are scared that they might lose a star player. If they do, they may not win a championship, or it might bring less ticket and merchandise sales. The fans allow this because they now think the player is smart. After all, this person is great at the game of whatever sport they play, so they OBVIOUSLY should tell us how to solve world peace, or better yet concoct a formula for the fuel mixture in the rocket going to the space station.

THIS IS NOT THEIR STAGE!!!! They play a sport and although some athletes are highly intelligent in other facets of life, their purpose on this stage (that is not theirs) is to play the game. Do not speak and do not prophesy. Who lied to these athletes and told them that we care about anything else, other than what they do in their sport? WE DID because we keep buying the tickets to the shit show!!!!

As fans, our coddle culture of sports has shown these athletes that they can do or say anything they want, as long as they are playing for "our team." Once they leave "our team," we burn their jerseys and renounce their very name. NOW all the bad that they have done (drugs, beatings, sexual harassment) is looked at as grotesque, and we drag their name through the dirt. We have shown them that it is ok to do as they want, as long as it is on our terms, and we will support them if "our team" is winning or going to the championship. OUR CULTURE has developed this attitude and arrogance in the athlete. Go back in time and watch athletes of yesteryear play and listen to what they said. They played the game and did commercials. Very rarely did you see one step out on "what they believe" and put their career or team respect in jeopardy.

Our culture has allowed the sport to take "our stage" away from us, and given it up to a thought process that makes the "athlete" more important. Back in the day, people said "Babe Ruth" was bigger than the game..........NO HE WASN'T, because without "the game" he was flipping burgers at Mickey D's!! (ok…maybe he got promoted to fries) but either way, he was not bigger than the game, AND NEITHER ARE THE ATHLETES OF TODAY!!!!

LET ME EXPLAIN……what I mean by "our stage" as I say this over and over in this book. "Our stage" is what we paid to watch. When we pay to see a concert, a Broadway show, or a ball game, we pay for a platform for the musicians, performers, and athletes to use. WE PAY to be entertained in some way. Without the money we put in, that "platform" would not have anyone on it. There would be no funds for that platform to operate and therefore would remain empty. Whether it be on

Broadway, a concert, or a playing field shown on TV, IT IS OUR STAGE!!!! We paid for it.

Getting back to our culture in sports, as humans we love to be entertained. We love a good show or a good story. We have allowed these athletes to tell the "story" AS THEY PLEASE without holding them accountable, and yet we paid for the book. Does this make sense? It is your money that pays them to play the game. What part of that money allows them to be arrogant and believe they have power? I'll tell you what part.

There is an initial investment of "your money" or a "funding" you might say, that is a symbol of your gratitude for them being on "your team." As long as they perform, you will further the funding of YOUR STAGE. If they do not perform, then you are less likely to watch or go to a game, therefore defunding YOUR STAGE. When an athlete becomes arrogant and uses YOUR STAGE for their personal agenda, why do you keep funding that stage? Why would you allow an athlete to use the hard-earned money that you worked for to feed your family and live the life "you" want, to speak "their" agenda? CULTURE!!!! We overlook it, or to use a better term we "put up with this BULLSHIT." At this point, we should be thinking of this as a business deal instead of a game. WOULD YOU ALLOW a co-worker to steal your proposal that you worked tirelessly on, only to call it their own? Would you allow a co-worker to take the credit and get paid on a sale you made? I would hope NOT!!!! Then why do you allow your employee (athletes) to do as they want on your stage with your hard-earned money?????

This is where I say, "F YOUR CULTURE." I QUIT!!!! I REFUSE to allow these assclowns to run my show. I refuse to let any athlete use my stage to further their career other than playing the sport. Any political agenda, even if it aligns with the way I think should never be allowed on my stage. Any personal agenda, unless it is about doing your job as an athlete, should never be allowed on my stage. These athletes think they are the only ones good enough for that stage, and yet forget about the thousands behind them trying to take their spot. STOP IDOLIZING THE INDIVIDUAL and be true to the game.

Once an athlete taints the game with outside influences REPLACE HIM OR HER. Once your stage has been stolen or adulterated, DEFUND THE PLATFORM!!!! (Remember me saying the "bottom line would come up again? NBA viewership is down 43% and continuing to slide due to the league and its athletes arrogance in speaking their mind on issues OTHER THAN BASKETBALL) These athletes are YOUR employees. If there is no money coming in, their salaries disappear. Who pays their salaries???? YOU DO!!!! (NFL VIEWERSHIP IS DOWN SIGNIFICANTLY, due to the league letting these assclowns kneel for the National Anthem……HEY FUCKERS…. we've been playing that song since the sport's infancy and there is NOTHING racist about it, but you are just now protesting???? THIS SOLIDIFIES MY STATEMENT THAT THEY GOT THROUGH SCHOOL ON THEIR ATHLETIC ABILITY ALONE)

IT IS THE PEOPLE'S STAGE!!!! Once these athletes started bad-mouthing the National Anthem EVERY RED-BLOODED AMERICAN should have defunded their stage (I certainly did and have not looked back) but some sheeple are weak and will continue to follow their athlete Gods.

IT'S NOT ABOUT WHAT THEY THINK!!!! It is about how they dribble and shoot the ball. It is about how they run, catch, or throw the ball. It is about how they hit or kick the ball. Have you noticed that hockey and golf are about the only sports left where the athletes focus on their job, and perform "the game" on your stage? The other sports have grown arrogant and believe that you will continue to fund your stage as they speak out against your freedom, along with any other political agenda they have. They know you are WEAK, and they know you will continue to fund the stage, and you have proven them CORRECT. DO YOU KNOW WHY????? BECAUSE YOU ARE SHEEP!!!!!!

I am one of those people that truly enjoys sports and watching athletes do superhuman shit. I am also one of those rare humans that can cut it off when the winds of change go awry and turn the game into something it was not supposed to be. When it is not just a game anymore and I have to worry about what bullshit I have to listen to from these arrogant bastards, then I no longer fund the stage. IF YOU WERE TO DO THE SAME, we would have games being played as they should, without fear of athletes opening their pie holes to tell you they know better than you! But the weak will follow.

This world is a business ladies and gentlemen. You need to start thinking about every transaction you make as a business deal. NO EMPLOYEE would be allowed to voice their open opinion about religion or political views in the workplace without being reprimanded, unless that employee is a pro athlete. PROVE ME WRONG!!!!

Stop the culture of "oh, it's ok that they say what they say, because he or she is on my team," kind of crap. Stop letting athletes invest your money for their agenda. Change the culture of sports back to a game. It was once a game that was played by grateful athletes knowing that their hard work paid off. It has now been weaponized to sway you one way or the other on everything else but the sport itself. You are lucky to watch a game these days without being raped by agenda on jerseys, floors, fields, or commercials. We let this happen to us. WE let sports take our investment and adulterate it for their needs.

"F" the sports culture of today's athletes. I will not fund this business knowing I have the power to make a difference. If they do not like America, then stop paying them in American money. China owns 20% of the NBA.......20%!!!! How many of you knew that? They have more alliance with China than they do to their own country and the people that made them what they are!!!! Your money goes to the athlete, the athlete's loyalty goes to "China."

KEEP FUNDING "YOUR TEAM." Keep letting these athletes say and do what they want, and you will no longer have the opportunity to watch super-human shit. They will wreck the stage so badly that it is not usable anymore.

Example: The top car racing circuit.... those ass-clowns forgot what country, much less what category of Americans funded that stage. They are digging their grave as we speak. The Pro Football's bottom line is also taking a shit for similar reasons. (I hope this new division that some of the seasoned race car drivers are starting takes off and sends stock cars packing to the obsolete graveyard, for no other reason than that they got cocky and way too greedy.)

With respect to athletes that do play the game and are great role models for kids and adults alike, thank you for staying true to form. We need more athletes like you as leaders. Do not let the troubled ones sway you. HOLD THE LINE!!!!! AND P.S................... THERE IS NO SUCH THING AS "STREET CRED"

BY NOW......You are either close to having a grand mal, or you totally agree with me and are enjoying this read. Go make some popcorn, because this shit is getting good and I am going to lay it the "F" out for you in these following chapters.

BUSINESS!!!!

CEOS............. WHAAAAAAAAAAAAAAT KIND
of OBVIOUS do you not understand regarding
business 101?

RULE #1.... SELL YOUR PRODUCT!!!!

SELL.......... YOUR............DAMN..........
PRODUCT!!!!!! Business 101 has never, ever changed. It
does not say "sell your product to certain people." It does
not say "sell your product to only white, black, Latino, or
Asian cultures." It does not say sell your product to just
men or just women." IT SAYS, "SELL YOUR PRODUCT!"
So why is it that CEOs and owners of big businesses think
they are untouchable, and won't face repercussions regarding the things they say?

Example: The CEO/OWNER of a large coffee company said FOR FACT.... "We don't WANT your conservative money!" What kind of jackassery is this? Why would
any "business" person (that wants their products to do
well) want to cut out 30-50% of their clientele? DOES

THIS MAKE ANY SENSE TO YOU? *IF IT DOES, then you were probably a crayon eater in school, so it's no surprise.*

There are multiple examples like this over recent history, and it is mind-boggling, and not just over politics. Some fast-food chains back their employees when they refuse to serve police officers. Are you kidding me? When did we allow the employees to take over? (hold that thought…I will answer that for you soon) This "culture" is pretty much what this book is based on for the most part.

(My opinion, there should be a registry of who doesn't like cops and refused to serve them. When those individuals call the cops, it keys the 911 operator and they do not answer the call. FAIR IS FAIR RIGHT???) REAP THE REWARDS OF ASSCLOWNACY!!!!

Other companies are teaching their employees to be "LESS OF THEIR COLOR." There aren't enough cuss words in the English language to say what I want about this Fucktardation!!!! It was easy for me to switch to the red, white, and blue can after that INCREDIBLY IMBECILE DECISION!!! What also gets me is restaurants that still carry the product of the "be less" company, while at the same time teaching their employees not to be racist or firing them because they are!!!! But we continue to buy from them…………SHEEP!!

MULTIPLE companies have started letting their employees wear clothing and other items that state only one color of life matters, and have found themselves in trouble with their clientele due to boycotts. SELL YOUR PRODUCT!!! I do not care if you get a HUGE tax break or whatever was promised to you. Do not let your employees wear anything but the uniform. This goes back to "IT IS NOT THEIR STAGE." "FRANKS AND BEANS!"

What have we become when our businesses think it is ok to get involved in the political game? Why is it that CEOs and businesspeople with highly touted degrees listen to advisors, that listen to managers, that listen to snowflake employees (that do not want to work anyway)? Why is it that "common sense" of how this world was built business-wise, does not ring true to these people any-more? When did we cut our nuts off as business owners and bow down to a bunch of kids that want you to pay for their college and provide coffee and massage chairs in the workplace? I keep hearing, "Employees these days are different. They want certain things, and we have to treat them with kid gloves." WHAT??? Shit in one hand and want in the other and see which one weighs more!!!! I do not care if they "want" certain things in the workplace. This "coddle culture" in which everyone gets a trophy has led to mediocrity in business. You have workers that can coast through their jobs, sip their lattes all day, and drive their electric cars home, ALL THE WHILE expecting to make six-figure incomes because they have an underwater basket weaving, liberal art, performing arts degree with a minor in "sociology and gender studies," sitting on the bean bags you bought for them to be comfortable. ASSCLOWNS!!!! *(forget run-on sentence, that was a run-on paragraph)*

Do you know who the main culprit to this disorganization of business is??? HR.... HUMAN RESOURCES. HR has taken what employees "want" and disguised it as a "critical need" to CEOs to stay compliant with workforce equality or whatever the HELL they want to call it these days. HEY CEOS......IT IS A TROJAN HORSE!!! Your HR thinks they need to come up with policies to "keep their jobs" and make it look like they are productive. All they have done for you is delegitimized your ownership and now the inmates run the asylum. You guys are so worried about the "employee experience" that you have lost touch with the experience of the ones that pay you................. THE CUSTOMERS!!!!!

(By the way......you can agree or disagree with whatever I say. I honestly could give two shits and will not lose a minute of sleep over it....... now keep reading!!!!)
But........if you have common sense then this book should ring true to you.

CEOS AND EXECUTIVES are worried about the "numbers" much more than they ever will be about the people. This is why they are letting the employee take over their very own businesses. PAY ATTENTION!!!

Example: I worked for a major airline in Atlanta as a gate agent. We got CRUSHED daily. We had two-man gates (2 gate agents working the flight). The flight attendant crew was tired or just short of what they needed to cut costs (skeleton crew.) We had to work down overbooked flights every single flight and sometimes fit a 767 full of people because of an "equipment change" (the different plane being used), into an MD88. So, you are talking about a plane that holds 250 people or more that is over-booked already and put them into the "equipment change" of one that only holds 155 passengers. We used to call "A" concourse at the Atlanta airport "the killing fields." Anyway....we were usually getting our asses handed to us every flight. BUT WHEN THE CEO WAS GOING TO FLY OUT............... we had five-man gates, 2 extra flight attendants, and a fresh crew with 4 redcoats within 20 feet of the desk at all times. THIS is exactly what I mean when I tell you that CEOs do not really want to know the people and what they must go through. TROJAN HORSE!!! *(I applaud the men and women of this airline and you know who you are "BIG D." You are all ROCKSTARS in my book. AS FOR THE LEADERSHIP......you need an*

ID to get on your plane so why not to vote??? Business 101 escapes you.....I personally boycott you now)

As the CEO of my company, I am going to sneak up on your ass and see how my company is really running. I am going to the break room at ONE A.M. to talk to the employees and ask them to lay it out. I WOULD WANT TO KNOW!!!!!

General sales meetings!!! If there ever was a smoke and mirrors type play in business, this is it. This is where the top brass brings you all together and tries to show you how much they care after spending the last three months barely saying a word to you at all, much less giving you an uplifting pat on the back for anything. (don't worry the employees see right through it) It is kind of like when politicians need your vote because an election is coming up. They call your phone daily and ask for funding or your vote. Once the election is over, they do not call your phone at all. NOT EVEN TO SAY THANK YOU!!! TROJAN HORSE!!!

These quarterly general sales meetings are CRAP!!! IT'S ALL FLUFF!!!! If you did not know already, your employees don't like them, except for the kiss asses that want you to pick them for your hopscotch tournament. PICK ME!!!! PICK ME!!!! While all the other employees are sitting there calling bullshit on everything you are "pretending" to care about. It is all crap. YOU know it and WE KNOW IT FOR SURE. You have sales execs, HR, and regional managers all get up and fluff how their team is doing. You even invite anyone that wants to share their experience on how they helped a customer up to the front of the room. So, when "Sally" hears this, she gets up and tells you how she helped her customer because she wants to be captain of the hopscotch team. She says,

"When I saw my customers sales were down and I wanted to cheer them up, I made a bunch of cupcakes and put cute little bows on them" **(imagine my voice going up several octaves while saying that).**

Then everyone claps and the execs say "Oh how awesome that is Sally? THAT is helping your customer make it." "NO....NO IT'S NOT SALLY!!! YOUR CUPCAKES SUCK AND THEY ARE GOING TO CHOKE ON THOSE SHITTY LITTLE BOWS SO SIT THE FUCK DOWN WITH YOUR SIDEWALK CHALK AND LET'S GET THIS MEANINGLESS MEETING OVER WITH" is what the other employees are saying that need to TRULY get on the phone with their customers or go visit them to DO THEIR JOB!!!!! *(was that a run-on sentence? DEEEEEEEEEEP BREATHE to get air in your lungs so you can read more of this masterpiece)*

Another example: I worked for a major food distributor and during my whole time there my "VP OF SALES" might have been the most arrogant individual that I have ever worked under. This guy had Napoleon syndrome for sure (although he might have been shorter than Napoleon himself). This is a man who the employees did not trust. They did not want him on new account meetings (because he sat and texted the whole time), and he even told an employee not to get any more of a certain type of account because it did not help "his" numbers. GOD FORBID it helps the employee with their numbers, MUCH LESS THE COMPANY WITH SALES. All the while HR was informed of this and turned a blind eye. Scared they might lose their "Quan." *"SHOW ME THE MONEY AND I'LL COVER-UP ANYTHING YOU WANT" ~HR.*

When I was hired, this company touted how great their "culture" was. That was one of the main reasons I chose to work for them (also one of the final factors to write this book). If this is a "great" culture............ F YOUR CULTURE!!!! This company and its executives are "false flags" for the term leadership. Your culture is a mile below shit.

This is what I mean by CEOs not "really" wanting to know what is going on with their people as long as the numbers are good. So, when this sales exec. gets up in front of the General Sales Meeting and starts talking about teamwork and how much he cares and the "let me know what you need" bullshit.... the whole room is thinking "ASSCLOWN LIAR." Integrity is an essential part of running a good company....... wouldn't you think? CEOs DON'T THINK SO AS LONG AS THE NUMBERS ARE GOOD.

Businesses these days are looking for bodies. If you are not the right body, then they will find one. Turnover is higher now than it ever has been.

Companies used to train and guide the employee to help them succeed. They used to show employees how things are done and how different employees succeeded. They wanted to see their employees grow with the company and be there for many years. If employees messed up somewhere down the line, they counseled them and gave them more training. Nowadays companies do not even want to know your name because they know that you will not be there long enough; and BETTER YET, they do not "want you" to be there too long. HR sees this and instead of protecting the employee like they are supposed to, they sell their soul for the dollar and do WHATEVER the company wants. Then they "guide" the company in the process of legally letting them go. Money over morals no doubt!!!! *(HR has been weaponized to back the company and forget the employee)*

Companies know that as you get tenure this means raises, and they can just get the new guy to do your job for less wages. They start to push you out with new rules or whatever they can come up with, and when you are gone the next guy gets all your accounts and costs the company less in salary. DO YOU GET IT YET?? COMPANIES DON'T CARE!!!! No matter how good you "were" if you are not cutting it now.... SEE YA!!! They care about the numbers.... not humans.

I am not saying all companies are bad. There are many good companies out there that expect the best out of their employees and most of the time get the best. This is called "LOYALTY."

Loyalty is what every single CEO should be looking for and every single manager should be trained on getting from the employee. You want a great "culture" in your business? Try working on getting "loyalty" and you will have the greatest culture on earth.

I KNOW FOR A FACT I can walk into your company as a new employee and get more loyalty from my coworkers in a week, than most of the managers have acquired over years. I do it all the time and it is easy. It amazes me how managers literally fail at this simple phase of management.

How do you get loyalty? Well, it is not by giving your employees bean bags and all the fucking coffee they can drink. This does not cultivate loyalty, it cultivates "expectancy" and a shit ton of bathroom breaks. (A plumber's dream).

These are the kids that you see in the grocery store throwing a fit in front of their mom to get a toy. THEY EXPECT IT!!! The loyal kids are those jumping into the basket and pummeling the kid throwing a fit, so "their" mother does not have to hear the tantrum their trash family has created. JUST KIDDING!! The loyal kids are the well-behaved kids that walk quietly and "speak" to their parents respectfully because they know they are taken care of. WHAT KIND OF EMPLOYEES (KIDS) DO YOU HAVE?? I thought so.

With today's culture, these kids expect to have certain things in order for them to grace your company with their presence. Do you want to hear about two great companies that created endless loyalty from me toward them? I have a couple quick stories about two companies that I will forever be indebted to with the lessons they taught me.

FIRST STORY....... I was recruited to manage a 24/7 restaurant in Atlanta. There was a store on every exit and many more all over Georgia. Never having managed a restaurant before, I gave myself one year with them to see if the restaurant biz was for me or not. After training with what might have been one of the best managers I have ever trained under, they gave me my store. It was the worst store in Atlanta. It was a shithole. It was the last place in the rankings in Atlanta. I hired and tried to get the right crew, but it was not easy. I worked 18-20 hours a day sometimes just to make sure my customers were getting what they deserved. My district manager at the time (Dave) was an awesome dude. This guy was young, and he would see me get angry or anxious when we started getting busy and, in the weeds, (getting smashed with customers). I always felt that my customers having to wait for their food would not bid well for me. Dave would tell me, "Just cook. No matter how busy you get, just cook. Don't look at the people, it will all come together, I promise." This guy was insanely good. That phrase has stuck with me since then and whenever I get in the weeds no matter what I am doing I tell myself to "just cook." I believe he is the Executive VP for them now and well deserved.

(Dave, if you read this, your talks made a huge difference in my life……. Thank you.)

One night we were in the weeds and were on a wait. The dishes were not getting done and we were doing our best just to get by. I see a limo pull up outside and the CEO/

OWNER of the company hops out in a full-blown tux-edo, obviously going somewhere important. I could see his wife sitting in the limo as well, dressed to the nines. He walked into my store and all I could think was, I am getting fired right now. He takes off his tux jacket, rolls up his sleeves, and tells me, "I was riding by and saw you could use some help." WTF? He then started washing my dishes. Once they were caught up, he asked if I needed anything else and I told him thank you very much and he was on his way. LOYALTY PEOPLE!!!!!! I will not only eat there every chance I get, but I hold the door open for people coming and going to help customers have a good experience. DO YOU GET IT YET?

I ended up bringing that store to the #2 position for many months in several different categories. When my year was up, I resigned knowing it was not for me. That day I got a call from every single ranking member of that organization begging me to stay and telling me I could pick my store. The restaurant biz was not for me, but THIS company CULTURE nailed it.

SECOND STORY.... I got into the bodybuilding business by way of sports supplements. Anything from protein powders to capsules. Anything you would see in nutrition shops or online sites, I did it. My first company was strictly commission. The FDA had a hard-on for this company (probably because their products worked better than any on the market) and would always give them a rough time. When I started, all their products were embargoed for testing, and we did not know when we were getting it back and we could not make more. I was given a landline phone, a phone book, (what is a phone book?), and a computer and told to "go." They wanted me to call stores all over the US and around the world if I could find them. I was selling products without even knowing when we would be able to ship them. For the first three months, I was making about $300 per month (as a 1099 employee). $300 PER "MONTH!!!" I lived off protein powder and an appetite suppressant every day. I would have one scoop of protein two times a day and that was my food source. The appetite suppressant kept me from thinking about being hungry. There were nights I would sleep in my truck because I did not have enough money for gas to get home and back. I would be the first one there and the last to leave every day. I would follow the sun across the United States, calling every store, in every state that I could find to build my business. I was not making it and contemplated giving up. I guess the owner observed what was going on because he gave me a bonus just for sticking with it. He gave me $350. He might as well have given me a million dollars. All thoughts of quitting left my mind as I was instantly "LOYAL" to this man.

A few weeks later our products were released and my first full year I ended up making $30K. By my third year, I was making $300K per year because I was given a chance and was hell-bent on making this work because of my loyalty to the owner and the "want" to build his business. Because of that chance, I buy their products to this day. They also make the best products on the supplement market hands down. They are a very High Tech supplement company that makes THE best supplements in the biz. (hint hint….if you take supplements…this is the company to buy from)

I ended up walking away from that company due to an offer that was made to me for partial ownership in another. The owner of this supplement company is a huge part of my success in life. He taught me compassion along with the need to make sure you are watching your employees, even when they do not think you are.

LOYALTY MAKES GOOD EMPLOYEES. LOYALTY MAKES GOOD "CULTURE," and it also makes GREAT AMBASSADORS for your business if and when the employee decides to leave. Makes sense huh? No shit…you are damn right it does but we just do not get it anymore.

THE CUSTOMER IS ALWAYS RIGHT!!!

BIGGEST BUNCH OF BULLSHIT THE GREATEST salesman in the world sold big business.

I take that back, "2nd" greatest salesman. The greatest salesman ever was the guy who invented the pet rock! If you can get someone to buy a painted rock that came in a brown thin cardboard box coddled with some fake straw for $3 and change, YOU are the greatest of all time. This guy unloaded 5 million rocks that cost him one cent a piece in 6 months and walked away with 15 million dollars.................IN THE '70s. GOOD FOR HIM... MAKES ME HAPPY!!!

Anyway.... if you are a business that still plays the game of "the customer is always right," I'm about to light your world up. You are going to cry like a little girl that just wet her pants on the playground when I tell you how wrong you are!!! ARE YOU READY? GET YOUR TISSUE!!!

Why is it that we believe everything we hear and make it the "gospel?" Why do businesses adopt a mind-set due to someone just "saying" a phrase? We dub those that came up with the phrase as great salesmen because THEY were successful. YES, it takes a different breed of people and thought process to execute sales and be good at it. Anyone can try it, but there are a ton of people who suck at it.

Made famous in the early twentieth century, "the customer is always right" referred to success in business being dependent on "happy customers." This was not supposed to be all customers are right, and as a business we should take their shit. There is a point that you need to tell the customer to pound sand and let him or her become a pain in the ass to your competitor. The customer is wrong more times than they ever are right about how YOUR business should be run. The experience you give them as a business is what makes it "right" for them to come back, or even want to for that matter. You as a business owner or CEO should be concentrating on the experience, or better yet the story your customer is privileged to. You should not be concentrating on kissing their ass because they did not like your food but ate all of it anyway. You need to be focused on their loyalty as a "profitable" customer. (Remember what I told you about life being a business transaction. When the customer is no longer profitable, kick them to the curb)

Businesses today have taken this phrase and embedded it into their little brains that all customers need to be happy with their business. Guess what? THEY DON'T!!! There is a percentage of customers that you will never please. Whether it is not the right product for them or they are just assclowns that are unhappy with everything, YOU CAN'T PLEASE EVERYONE and the sooner you realize this, the more profits you will have.

I worked for a national pizza chain and delivered pizzas for a while when I was fed up with fake corporate culture. (do not dismiss running pizza. I made 40K a year doing it) Anyway, it is always the same group of people that complain the pizza is never right. It was burned, or there was not enough cheese. They don't tip the driver.... EVER!!! You did not make it fast enough when the whole city ordered at the same time on Super Bowl Sunday!! I call them the Ten Percenters.

Ten Percent of customers are just not happy and never will be, with anything your company does or with the product itself. WHY IS IT we hang on to them begging them to make our lives miserable? If companies would realize that telling these people they are NO LONGER IN DANGER of ever doing business with us again, and to go to a competitor, they will. What are the benefits of this action? Now…. your employees are happier. Your food cost goes down, and profits go up. MOST OF ALL you have created LOYALTY from your employees. They just saw you tell a customer that gives them hell all the time and never tips, to go somewhere else and not to return (in a nice way of course). THERE IS NOT ONE THING WRONG WITH THIS. Oh, but we are afraid to get a bad online review. You as a company are allowed to respond to that review and lay out that they were given more than enough chances to behave, and being that they refused to, you kindly asked them to shop somewhere else. When I personally see a reply from a company like that, I instantly give that company my business. Why? Because I know you just stood up for yourself, your employees, and every other business out there that wants to do what you just did and now sees it can be done. By the way…when you send a customer to a competitor, they become their problem child. As time goes by these customers run out of places to shop because everyone has told them to pound sand. They then either calm their asses down and behave, or go without. Either way, you don't give a damn anymore because they are not your problem.

When they do try to come back, you welcome them with open arms as if they were a new customer at arm's length. You give them great customer service and maybe throw something extra to them to regain their LOYALTY. But it is different this time. They now know you are not afraid to let them walk.

THERE HAS TO BE FEAR TO STOP A DISRUPTIVE ACTION. People have to know there are consequences. If there are no consequences for customers acting a fool, they will keep doing it and try to get away with more and more. (Same idea with Antifa….if we keep letting them burn the place down and do what they want it will continue. But, if we hand their ass to them, I promise they will stop their shit no matter how much they are being paid to be disruptive….GET IT? *DAAAAAAAAAMNIT GOT OFF SUBJECT WITH MY PASSION….please continue!!!*)

This leads back to CEOs not paying attention to their people and "HR" fluffing your pillow on policies they pull from their ass only to kiss yours as the CEO. TROJAN HORSE!!!!

CEOs….do me a favor. A college degree is fine but when you are making policies either have that "degree" working in the position for 6 months or ask the people that actually do the job. More times than not CEOs of companies will rely on some 22-year-old degreed child who paid a shit ton for a piece of paper, rather than ask someone that has done the job for many years if the idea will work or not. THINK ABOUT IT!!!! Do you as a CEO ask the custodian how to do "your" job? NO…. you had a team of executives through life that have trained you and have DONE THE JOB to help you become the CEO you are today!!! PROVE ME WRONG!!!

(PLEASE NOTE: you need to bonus that custodian because he's cleaning up the latte cups and fluffing the bean bags of the employees you are coddling because you don't make them clean up their own mess like their parents never did either)

The "culture" of believing the customer is always right, is insane. Of course, the customer is needed. Who are you going to sell your product to if you do not have any? But to champion a thought that a customer cannot be given his or her walking papers is archaic at best. "F" THAT CULTURE FOR SURE. Grow your business with the loyal customers and employees that you CAN make happy and in turn make your company even more profitable.

Any business that is coddling its employees at an unhealthy level is going to fail outright or fail to hit the highest peak possible. You will end up having expectant children wanting more and more that you cannot provide. Work is work!!!! You can have great benefits for your employees, but you need to pull the reins on your HR, and you need to be on the ground floor analyzing if you run a resort, or if you run a business. Depending on how you answer, you are still paying the worker to get the job done. Right now, it is done on their time in between coffee breaks instead of yours.

BUSINESS HAS TO CHANGE BACK!!!! "F" YOUR CULTURE of business the way it is run today. This generation of "everyone gets a trophy" children has come of age and now you have mediocrity in business instead of competitive natured employees. You think you have a different kind of employee and that YOU need to change for them when you do not. You have a human that has been taught to be lazy their whole life, coddled by their mommy, and frankly has never had anyone kick their ass enough to get out and fight for something.

They expect you to coddle them, because so far everyone in their life has. CONGRATS…THEY CONTROL YOU NOW!!!! They have snipped your balls right off and took the sack with them because you were gifted a TROJAN HORSE by your HR that has deceived you into thinking "this is critical for your company's success." IT'S NOT……….. IIIIIIIIT'S NOT!!!!

What do you think your top performers are thinking? They sit there and see the underperformers, or the "mediocrity" get the same bean bags, coffee, and massage chairs they do. Yes, they get more pay because they sell more product, but what other benefits are they getting that the "mediocrity" is not having to work harder to get? DO YOU GET IT???

If you run your business then run the damn thing. Get back to competing with other businesses and rewarding DRIVEN SUCCESS!!! How many bonuses have you had to payout if someone gets to a certain level?? You ask your managers "what is it going to take to get these guys to sell?" I remember when employees were hungry and did not need to be bought. I remember when they wanted to be #1 in sales in whatever they sold for bragging rights alone. Of course, the money came with being #1, but walking into the office knowing you were #1 meant the world.

Run your business. SELL YOUR PRODUCT............ to everyone. Stay out of the political arena and do your job. The only people that care about who you vote for ARE THE CUSTOMERS YOU LOSE by choosing who they do not like. LET ME SAY THAT AGAIN BUT LISTEN THIS TIME. "THE ONLY PEOPLE THAT CARE ABOUT WHO YOU VOTE FOR ARE THE CUSTOMERS YOU LOSE BY CHOOSING WHO THEY DO NOT LIKE!!!!!!!!!!!!!" The ones that agree with you are not going to buy more to make up for that loss. They are just going to keep buying, but meanwhile you lose half your customer base because you opened your pie hole with an agenda that nobody needs to hear!!!!!

SELL YOUR PRODUCT...............BUSINESS 101!!!!

This is where I say "F" YOUR CULTURE to business and how it is run today. You tout a "great culture" to lure employees in, but you are not getting the right ones. The employees that are looking for never-ending free coffee, bean bags, and massage chairs ARE NOT the employees you need for your business to be competitive in this world market; Or at least not as competitive as it could be. But HEY, who knows, you might be one of those half-assed CEOs that wants a bean bag too.

Start rewarding DRIVEN SUCCESS from employees that bust their asses and learn your business. YOU OWN THE BUSINESS....YOU SHOULD RUN IT!!!! Like I said before, are you running a resort or a business? The word culture is so overused anymore even HR is trying to come up with another bullshit line to stuff in their Trojan Horse. Get back to developing good people. Learn how to create loyalty, not only to your business but employee to employee. When employees see the good in people that are trying, and they help them learn..........EVERYONE WINS!!!

You should see me pounding on this keyboard! I'm so excited, I might have to take some seizure meds myself! Are you still with me? STANDBY, this next chapter is about THE HUMAN RACE and I am going to offend alllllllllllllll you fucktards that think mommy and daddy were right to let you live in the basement until you are 40 playing video games all day diddling to porn because your insecurities keep you from venturing out to be "normal" and part of a functioning society. (another run-on sentence? Screw it…. I said it all in one breath……….. SCORE!!!!!!)

HUMANITY... OR THE LACK THEREOF!!!!

WE HAVE CRUCIFIED THE HUMAN RACE!!

Get ready because I am going to cover some shit that some of you will not like. BUT IF YOU LOOK AT FACTS........... you should all agree with the points I am trying to get across. If you think I am "racist" (such an overused word by morons and media scapegoats) with any of this, you are not truly reading my words. If you know me (which you don't) I do not care if you are black, white, pink, or polka-dotted. I do not care if you are from Earth or FREAKING MARS.......it does not bother me one bit. Gay or straight I do not care. READ THE FACTS AND OPEN YOUR DAMN MINDS UP FOR GOD'S SAKE. We were given the gift of being the smartest species on the planet, and yet we are trying to even the playing field by dumbing ourselves down.

(Holy shit, where do I start? Screw it .... get on this roller coaster and strap in..........We 'gone fer a riiiide!!!!!)

How is it as humans we can be 180 degrees opposite from another human in almost everything we believe? The majority of us have ten fingers, ten toes, the same limbs, and the same shit on our face with two eyes, a nose, and a mouth. We all have the same organs inside of us, (or we are supposed to) we have the same kind of brain matter, (some are smaller and some just don't use it) and WE ALL BLEED RED, but yet we are sooooooooo different. How does this happen?

How as humans, have we let "the powers that be" make us believe that down is up and up is down? That good is bad and bad is good. What chemical makeup keeps some of us knowing the power of common sense and others being absolutely delusional in their thought process? What has happened to believing FACTS!!!? CULTURE IS WHAT HAPPENED!!! (and a shitty one at that)

We have dumbed down our culture so much over the past fifty years that we are one commercial away from window licking. We have let social media and THE MEDIA tell us how to think and be dependent on them to the point of crippling any and all imagination or cognitive thought. As humans, we are supposed to EVOLVE, yet all we have done is DISSOLVE humanity.

Parents of my generation were the first to foot this blame. They did not like how they were paddled as kids, made to do chores and work for a living. So, they vowed to never put their kids through such "torture." CONGRATS MOM AND DAD, now you are footing the bill for two generations that have been coddled and are easily brain-washed. Your kids are so into themselves and their needs that they have forgotten how to help others and have empathy toward anything. Your kids were brought up with video games as a babysitter because you were too LAZY to have anything to do with them, and you did not want to be bothered. So, you shoved a phone in their hand to keep them quiet and let the village do the job you were supposed to. Guess what…. the village became their parents. You became the enabler. You were just there to bide time and keep them fed. Your kids were getting all the info they needed from social media, and it was not the "right" information. But "hey", how would you know??? You alone created the "it's all about me generation." Kids these days look more for "likes" from people they DON'T EVEN KNOW than from you the parent. Think about that. Your kids would rather get approval from a total stranger than to ever hear a word from your mouth! CONGRATS!!!

Kids are like pets. You still need to socialize them as they grow up or they become little assholes that cannot look up from their phone or say hello to a person they pass in the grocery store. Hell, your kids can't even make eye contact with anyone unless they know them, and even then, it's a toss up.

You were too busy to socialize your kids, so now your excuse is that "they are just introverted." NOT A FUCKING CHANCE!!!! The human race is supposed to be social. We are meant to socialize with each other, not "social media" with each other. We are meant to talk to one another, and laugh and touch each other *(not in a stranger danger type of way)*. There is no way in hell that your kid's whole generation in some strange way, suddenly became 85% introverts. The village has taken your God-given gift and manipulated their little minds the way THEY wanted them to grow. The internet not only babysat your kids, but it babysat you as well. You were so engrossed in the new age of technology that your kids no longer had "parents," they had siblings.

You were more of their friend than you ever were a parent. You lived on social media too, just like they did and forgot your priorities. "Likes" were more important to you than your kid's life and well-being were. How many people are "following" you was all you wanted to make your endorphins peak. You allowed them to talk back and live under your roof with no direction on where they were going in life. You allowed them to "stay as long as you want," for fear of your sibling leaving the roost and suffering by having to work for a living. This not only crippled them from growing up and being a functioning part of society, it crippled society, only to form sheeple.

ENTER the largest generation of followers in human history. We thought the hippies in the '60s were bad......this generation said, "HOLD MY BEER!!!"

They were given everything they could for free and now they want more. They want free coffee at work. They want taxpayers to pay for their college. They want, want, want, unknowing what society needs in order to function. You did not teach them economics. You relied on "the village" to teach them their idea of how money works. Because of this, these assclowns think that the government can just spend as they wish without understanding what taxes do and the effects of such overreach. They think that there is a never-ending supply of money that they should not have to work for. THEY ACTUALLY BELIEVE that the government cares for them so much that they raised minimum wage "just so they could live better." *(HEY KNOW IT ALLS.... the government raised the minimum wage so they could tax you more and get rid of the middle class!!!)* Because you gave them everything and never said "no," they believe anything and everything the media tells them. They believe that socialism is better than FREEDOM. ARE YOU KIDDING ME?!!! And yet you remain silent having never personally lived in a socialist world where people die trying to escape it to live in FREEDOM. *WE*

KEEP EATING THE FRUIT OF FREEDOM BUT YET WE HAVE STOPPED WATERING THE TREE!!!

Your kids would rather film someone getting beat up or killed than to render aid. Won't it be nice to watch your child getting their ass kicked or killed on the internet because someone wanted notoriety for filming it, versus saving a life? It is different when it happens to your child, isn't it? It is not right when it is your blood. But when it happens to someone else, we get on social media and repost it a hundred times to get "likes." Disgusting display for animals much less humans.

Your kids cuss the police over an agenda the media wants to portray instead of looking at the cold hard facts. FACTS…. that is a strange word. I am surprised I am not being called "racist" for using the term. *(The undeniable truth that something is what it is………FACTS!!!)* Yet the world will tell you differently and you will believe them. The media will beat a dead horse when a white cop kills a black man, but stays eerily silent when a cop of any race kills a white man. Why should it matter what color killed or was killed? They are both human…right? If you look at the FACTS instead of your media God, you might get a little smarter. If a cop kills someone LET THE LAW FIGURE IT OUT…. JUST AS YOU WOULD WANT A FAIR TRIAL IF YOU KILLED SOMEONE. Society today is so quick to be keyboard cowboys and suddenly become law experts, judge and jury. We are quick to call for fir-ing someone because the media enslaves you to only see snippets of the whole story. WHY DO YOU NOT HOLD "THEM" RESPONSIBLE?

Why is it that later when the TRUTH does come out, and we find out what really happened, we are too proud to back off our crucifixion of the wrongly accused and say we were wrong to jump to conclusions? We might lose our street cred, right? Like I said in prior chapters, most of you sit in the church pew on Sundays and worship your God and as soon as you get out of that pew you become hypochristians and forget all of it. Or do you sit in church just for show, and think God will not know your inner evil? GOOD LUCK WITH THAT!!!

Here is a quick lesson in facts for you. 95% of all perps that are shot and killed by the police (no matter what color) were probably not following the law....... I KNOW, I KNOW......hard to believe but I'm going to chalk that up to always leaning toward FACTS!!! Why don't you hear about the same color-on-color crime as you do about a white man killing a black man? Because you are sheeeeeeeeeeeeeeeeeep!!!!! It is not the Agenda. As long as it's the same "color" killing their own, it's ok. The media must keep us divided and against each other by constantly showing "racist cops killing another color." YES............ YOU ARE THAT STUPID AND HAVE PROVED IT!!!!

(why do we keep letting them divide us....no matter what color we are... WE.....ARE......HUMAN!!!! ACT LIKE IT!!!!)

I do not know if you ever paid attention when shit hits the fan. You and all your friends are running AWAY from danger when police are running TOWARD it so that you are safe, and they DON'T EVEN KNOW YOU, NOR DO THEY CARE WHAT COLOR YOU ARE. FIREMEN.... are running "in" the burning building to carry your fat ass out of it. CRAZY THOUGHT PROCESS HUH? Someone has to do it since you are too scared to. WE need to start ZEROING in on who the real racists are. We need to start calling out who the real evil humans are in this world. THE MEDIA!!!

The employees of Newspapers, TV, Magazines, Social Media, and Radio are humans too, but they are human puppets to the people that want to control you, and they are doing an amazing job. You are enslaved and yes, I said ENSLAVED by them and their brainwashing. You believe what they say to be true, or you are just too fucking stupid to realize the slave you are. *(when I say slave, it is not about color so calm your asses down. It's about humans(all humans) that don't think for themselves and are told what to think and do)*

The people on the news every night are just reading. They do not even know what they are saying because every news channel across the country is saying the EXACT SAME THING!!! Mind control is the game. CONSPIRACY THEORY?

That phrase is just another way they control you, by labeling ideas and information that expose the agenda, as a "conspiracy theory." The media likes to use the term "most Americans". The reality is most Americans have no knowledge of anything the media speaks about. It is a way for them to make you believe they know what they are talking about. So, If you think differently, then you are not like most Americans. TRUST ME…. I am far from "like" most Americans when the media says most "ANYTHING."

Colleges these days are breeding grounds for socialism, lying to your kids about how evil the United States is instead of giving facts, and teaching history on how we became the greatest nation in the world. (I didn't say we are a perfect nation, because we do have our problems and many of them) But you as a parent still send your kids to college with the delusion that they are getting an education. There is no longer an education by any grade of schooling. Teachers have sold their souls and become sheep to the teachers' union. I used to have a soft place in my heart for teachers, but seeing the curriculum they are required to teach and knowing that less than 1% gave up their position KNOWING it's wrong, I think they are all part of the problem. Selling their soul for a paycheck (and not a very good one) and a few months off in the summer is not worth the young lives they are KNOWINGLY corrupting. Teachers, you are teaching kids how to take tests instead of truly teaching them. The education system is so dumbed down and yet you are too weak to stand up for what is right. Congratulations "DAD," the degree your kids received is a piece of paper with a side of brain washing. *"Do you want some fries with that shake?"* PROVE ME WRONG!!!!!

What have we done to our children? You were all once children, and you expected to be guided correctly. You trusted that you were going to be. Why is it ok for you to give up on anything that is right? This is not an opinion. I have watched the downfall of the human race over the past 35 years and the decline is astonishing. We are smarter than this, or at least we used to be.

The media and politicians are so good at what they do, they will name a legislative act the "Education Bill" and you dumbasses won't even look at what it is and then question why your taxes went up 11% with NOT ONE PENNY going to "education." These people are experts on naming bills and acts which hide their true intent behind a false façade

Example: One of our presidents named a new law "The Patriot Act." This was touted as an act to keep us safe from terrorists after 9/11. IT'S BULLSHIT......when you read what it really is, it permitted the Federal Government to spy on everyday Americans using the justification of "national security." These are ways they slide things in to slowly take your freedoms from you BECAUSE YOU ARE TOO "EDUCATED" TO READ IT!!!!

Another example, this COVID-19 BULLLLLLLLLLLLLLLLLLLLLSHIT!!!! I am not saying the virus isn't real but watching the whole thing progress and regress at certain times is total crap. IT'S A MIND FUCKING is what it is. We are getting screwed people. The elites want a global reset, and it is not for the good of man but the control of mankind. You cannot have Thanksgiving. You cannot have Christmas. You cannot go to church, but you can fly in a tube for three hours with 10 people all within arms-length and you are ok. You can go to Big shopping stores and wear your nasty ass pajamas, but private businesses cannot open because this virus only hits the middle-class establishments and not the big players with all the money......DO YOU GET IT YET?????? (It's not about the virus...it's about the "fear" of the virus for the administration of the vaccine) MONEY AND CONTROL!!!!

SHEEEEEEEP!!!! When all our freedoms are gone what do you think happens next? You do not know because you were not taught TRUE HISTORY!!! You were lied to. How come we still have so many homeless (or what I like to call professional gypsy's) if COVID-19 is that bad? DO YOU GET IT YET???? OH….and the vaccine mandate. My body, my choice, But only if you are getting an abortion, right?…..FUCK OFF!!!

I am not saying we need to overthrow the government by any means. What I am saying is that your "leaders" have bought into this in hopes to have a place on the high altar when the "elites" take over. Pawns are all they are. They are doing the work for the greedy and they too will be put on the train to the death camps when it is all said and done (figure of speech). Why are the "leaders" that are enforcing the shutdown laws still getting paid when YOU ARE NOT??? (I really hope your eyes are opening up)

When are we going to stop eating our own? When are we going to stop and think "hmmm maybe he is right because what I have been fighting for hasn't gotten any better?" We need to stand up as humans. We need to stand up around the world and demand answers. "Why are you trying to keep us hating each other? Why do you keep saying one thing and then doing another?" When do we wake up and join forces NO MATTER WHAT COLOR, SEX, OR RELIGION, and get over this power-hungry bullshit?

We keep talking about equality, but the want for equality has been given a new meaning in this world. Greed and power are what each color or demographic wants. There is no such thing as equality of results or equality of opportunity anymore. Equality was once a dream had by a great man. Humans have pushed him aside and they are eating their own to get on top.

SOCIAL MEDIA

WHEN HAS IT EVER BEEN OK FOR SOMEONE
to stifle the media and dictate what can and cannot be said?
The First Amendment protects this from happening. Then
why is it ok for any social media platform or website to
stifle the posts or videos of any American? IT ISN'T OK!!!
But yet we sit back and allow them to do this. This goes
back to IT'S NOT THEIR STAGE. It might be their site
but without the people, they close their doors for good.
We keep funding a stage that erodes our free speech. No
matter what side you are on, we should all be upset at this
and demand answers.

We hold these sites and apps on a pedestal similar
to what we do with famous people and athletes. We are
willing to take all the bullshit they hand out like "you have
posted something against our community standards." So
we say, "uh oh...I better calm down or I'm going to be put
in social media jail." What do you think they are doing to
you? STIFLING YOUR FREEDOM OF SPEECH!!!! What

makes another human think they can tell you what you can say and what you cannot? Just because someone is offended does not make YOU the problem. It makes THEM the problem, and THEY need to deal with it. They can either not be around you or not read what you posted. Why is it that my offense to their actions is not as bad as their offense to my post? The whole thing is a tongue-twisted dictatorial takeover of our FREEDOMS!!! Some of you are now saying, "this crazy-ass book writer is going a little far calling it a dictatorial action." AM I??? We condemn what the Nazis did and yet we are doing identical things under a different name. You just do not know history well enough to put two and two together. (you probably do not know math well enough to add two and two either seeing how some of you were taught Common Core)

THERE'S ANOTHER ARGUMENT………Common Core math!! WHY? Give me one good reason this was ever needed. Give me SOMETHING that will explain to me why some assclowns got together and implemented this on a NATIONWIDE SCALE. (I'll go make some popcorn to give you time to come up with an answer)

The only reason it would go nationwide like it did, as quickly as it did, was AGENDA!!! They needed it for some reason. Do you want to hear my opinion on it? (you bought the book you might as well read it all)

IN MY OPINION, Common Core separates the family cohesion. Mom and Dad were taught the right way. Common Core fuckshit was taught to the kid. This made it impossible for parents to help their kids do their homework, leaving "the village" to be the parent, BUT YET the parents were obedient slaves and put up with this and did not say a word except posting on social media how disgusted they were. GREAT JOB!!! When stuff like this is implemented on this grand of a scale you need to IMMEDIATELY gather yourself and ask why? Stop posting on social media where nothing will be done. You need to write your congressman/woman and write your school boards and demand answers. But you won't............ SHEEP!!! (HOMESCHOOLING....CRAZY THOUGHT HUH?) BY THE WAY......WHERE WERE THE TEACHERS IN ALL OF THIS...THEY KNEW IT WAS CRAP, BUT THEY NEEDED A PAYCHECK........SELLOUTS!!!!!!

When do we stop watching the news? For me, it was fifteen years ago. I refuse to give ratings to these assclown puppets of the State. When the media has been weaponized to show only one view and not "report ALL NEWS," it is time to disengage. When you can put 100 news stations together in one week and they all say the exact same thing almost word for word in every part of the Country, there is an agenda of control. PROVE ME WRONG!!!!

Why am I amazed that most of you are sheep? Most of you don't even know how to operate your car blinker. (quick rant……. The blinker tells those around you that you either "want" to get over or are going to turn. IT DOES NOT…………mean that you are going to get over right now when it isn't clear, and when you hit it 10 feet before your turn. You're just an asshole) Make sure your blinker fluid is full…………SHEEP!!!

BACK TO THE GOOD STUFF!!!! *You are asking your-self, "why does this guy think we are that stupid?"*

Two answers:

1. 99% of you buy a car with your hard-earned money and leave the dealership sticker on the back giving them FREE advertisement. They made "you" buy the car and they made "you" advertise for them………. free!!!! (never mind most of you don't get it)

2. Looking at what is going on in the world around us……………..you ARE stupid!!!! (EXAMPLE: San Francisco is one of the most iconic and beautiful cities in the United States. You guys allow people to shit on the streets. You go out to eat where there is shit. You live where there is shit. YOU ARE DUMB AS SHIT……………for letting this happen. Yet your lawmakers don't let anyone shit around the places

they live right? Funny that the "commoner" is good enough for this SHIT. My opinion..........every single business should move out of San Francisco until they decide to clean up this SHIT!!!)

I say this in a friendly kind of way in hopes to wake you up and DO SOMETHING ABOUT IT. Realize that you are being used in almost every aspect of life. When are we going to wake up and "take the hard road" and get out of our comfort zone? Granted, most of you do not care. You just coast through life and do what you do. Trust me, it shows. The go-getters immediately stand apart in every single job, from the pizza delivery person to the nuclear scientist. The "good ones" stand out in every position. They not only stand out at work, but they stand out IN LIFE!!!!

Today, I made it a point to look into and observe every car that I came across driving. I wanted to see how many people were "talking" to their children?

I would say about 93% of the cars with kids in them, had their heads buried in their phones. I saw a few people talking and the kids were engaging in conversation. I even saw one lady beating her kid in the backseat with her shoe, ALL WHILE DRIVING................ollllllllllllllld school!!!!! God Bless Her!

When are we going to teach our kids that there is an amazing world out there to see? This is one of many reasons vehicles have windows. Your child's mind grows at a rapid pace. YOU must guide them. Teach them. Parenting is not easy, but you chose it (and thank you for choosing life) so get off your ass and put some knowledge into your family tree. When the roots can no longer soak up water the tree FALLS with the slightest breeze!!!

"F" humanity's culture, from raising kids to coddling sub-standard humans. We cannot continue down this path of humans that do not talk. If we stop engaging one another in social atmospheres, as companions and friends, or just in everyday life, we will begin to lose the identity of the human race. We cannot survive in silence and reclusiveness. We must be able to communicate in person with and to each other and truly process what is being said and shown to us.

SUMMARY

OHHHHHHHHHHHHHHHHHHHHH SHIT!!!!! I HAD TO put my wallet in my mouth for that last part so I wouldn't bite my tongue off while going into convulsions from the excitement of what I've written. If this book put you into a full-blown grand mal, made you throw up, or even made you realize that Poo Poo undergarments would have been a good thing to invest in before reading it..................
THEN I SUCCEEDED IN MY MESSAGE.

LET'S REVIEW.......

Religions...

Religions need to step up and expand their horizons. I'm not talking about succumbing to another religious belief system. I am talking about forming some sort of "code" with each other. A "pact" if I may say it like that. When there is an attack on other religions, all others need to form a shield of protection with them and defend each other's right to worship who we want. I'M NOT SAYING.....defend the church when priests are abusing children. When this happens there needs to be SWIFT and "FINAL" punishment if you know what I mean. (my opinion of course). (And don't think that it just happens in the Catholic religion… it happens in all of them so let's make sure you are true to your word when you judge and blame……………… hypochristians)

Christians need to become Christians again. They need to revisit what the "FAITH" stands for and I mean TRULY stands for. They need to not only think of the church's teachings but their own teachings in real life. When I say "Teachings," I mean how you act and teach others through your actions. You can say you are Christian all day long but do your actions and way of life reflect it??? WELL……. DO THEY??? You do not have to live a sterile life by any means. We are not perfect beings but if you sit through mass, preach it to family and friends, then do your best to live it as well. Only makes sense, right? GOOD TALK?

RANT COMING IN 3………………..2……………..… WTF ARE YOU MEGA CHURCH GOERS DOING? You want to talk about an assclown thought process. You guys listen to an orator on stage that can preach the Word. Someone that can deliver it so well it makes the hair grow on your legs and the hair on your back stand up with excitement. BLESS YOUR LITTLE HEARTS…………. you give money to someone that speaks well and asks for "money" more times than the IRS!!!!! YOU are one special kind of stupid to keep giving to a "PREACHER" that tells you "God says to give more money to him." WHAAAAAAAAAAAT THE FUUUUUUUUUUUUUUUUCK HAS MADE YOU SO STUPID? Why would you give a man that lives in a multimillion-dollar compound that much money?

If your "preacher" flies on a private jet, drives an expensive car like a Bentley or Ferrari, wears a watch that costs over $500, and delivers his/her sermon in a tailored suit that costs $1000 or more……. THEN YOU ARE GIVING YOUR MONEY TO SATAN!!!!! PROVE ME WRONG!!!! This Jackass is taking you for all you have. You are running from God if you put up with this lie and trust me, he is not chasing you.

How do you not see the writing on the wall? HERE IS A GOOD STORY FOR YOU……. There is a so-called "preacher" that said since he preaches the word all over the world, he wants the church to buy him a $70 million private jet. SAD THING IS……. the church did it. (guess who owns the church…………..HIM) If you are part of this FUCKTARDATION then you deserve everything you get. YOU bought HIM that plane……. not the church. (ask him to use it to go see your grandchildren and tell me what the answer is)

DO THIS…. tell your "preacher" that you are only going to give 10% of your "tithing" to the church. The other 90% is going to Christian charities of your choice. See what his/her reaction is to that? They will probably tell you that you are the "Devil" at that point. THIS ALONE will prove what I'm saying about your so-called "preacher." If you do not believe me…I can't help you with that.

Back to the summary of religions. As I said in one of the earlier chapters, if we don't Defend Heaven here on earth……………there won't be a Heaven to Defend. If you let the government tell you when and where you can hold service, then you are well on your way to an atheistic dictatorship. STAND UP………… STAND UP for what is right and what is written to protect us. Separation of Church and State………… DOES NOT MEAN that the church cannot be a part of the government. It means that GOVERNMENT CANNOT TELL YOU WHAT RELIGION YOU CAN AND CAN'T FOLLOW. DON'T LET THE ASSCLOWN LAWYERS "interpret" it to their agenda.

Athletes…..

I would like to see real athletes stand up for what is right. I'd like to see the ones that call themselves "men of God" actually rise to the occasion and stand up for his name. I'd like to see a group of them stand up for what was once a fun game and reintroduce that process back to the public. I'd like to see the poser athletes that have such a low self-esteem of themselves and need the attention in every facet of life to just PLAY THE GAME!!! Like I said before. This is the people's stage and WE pay these salaries. If you look at it that way (which is the correct way) then you will also know that WE pay the salaries of the owners and investors too. These dillholes cannot survive without us. THEY CAN'T! Bring the "game" back. Teach your kids to listen to what is right and not the agenda coming from the mouths of these fools. Tell them not to look at what is taped to their helmets, jerseys, or what kind of socks they have. SHOW THEM the truth. If one of these ingrates says something that is not true....SHOW YOUR KIDS THE FACTS!!!! Be a part of their life and start showing them ACTUAL right from wrong instead of letting them believe this crap. This is our stage. THE WORLD is our stage, and we control who succeeds on it and who doesn't. We pay everyone.... does that make sense? WE, the working men/women pay the salaries of everyone. (Let that sink in) We can also bankrupt any sport that wants to continue bastardizing YOUR STAGE!!!! You just have to want it badly enough to stop a culture you refuse to give up.

When the game is a game again and we have shown all pro sports that we just want to see THE GAME................. then..............IT'S ON LIKE DONKEY KONG and your team is going to whoooooooooooooooooop dat asssssssssssssssssssssssssss!!!!!

Business and CEOs.....

The higher-ups in business need to pull their little girl pants up and run their companies instead of HR and the snowflakes who are DELEGITIMIZING YOUR OWNERSHIP!!!! There is a really simple word. It's been around for thousands of years. "NO!" Believe it or not, you are allowed to use this word (and if your HR says you can't.....TROJAN HORSE). You as the CEO are allowed to tell your employees simply, no.

Start running your company so that you compete and thrive. If the employees want bean bags and massage chairs make them EARN IT!!!!(OR BUY IT THEMSELVES) You had to earn your position....why don't they? Get rid of Mediocrity in business and start rewarding Driven Success. Look for the employees that want to help you succeed and toss the others.

Start teaching your managers how to get LOYALTY from your employees. There is no greater word for a product than "loyalty." Hold true to your brand for ALLLLLL people. Do not segregate or choose who you sell to. Sell to everyone that wants your product. You are in business to sell your product.....act like it!!!

Get rid of this "coddle culture" environment and develop passion instead of breeding expectancy.

KEEP YOUR FUCKING PIE HOLE SHUT!!! You opening your mouth to tell the world what "you" agree with IS NONE OF OUR BUSINESS AND ONLY HURTS YOURS!!!! You can either work on getting "loyalty" from the masses or lose 40% of them because you thought it was cool to puke up a shit sandwich. BUSINESS 101....right?

"THE ONLY PEOPLE THAT CARE ABOUT WHO YOU VOTE FOR ARE THE CUSTOMERS YOU LOSE BY CHOOSING WHO THEY DO NOT LIKE!!!!!!!!!!!!!"

Pull the reins in on your HR. Their sole purpose is to protect your employees and the liability of your company. It is NOT to come up with ideas on how to coddle forty-year-old basement dwellers that still play Dungeons and Dragons or trade Pokemon cards.

Tell your worst customers to pound sand. I believe in customer service, but I also believe in customer(s) service. It has to be a two-way street. If the customer is no longer profitable both monetarily AND respectfully............. SEE YA!!!! There has to be consequences for disruptive behavior.

Learn who your employees are. These are humans that have chosen to work for you and build your company. You may never know them by name but damnit how about walking in their workplace every now and then to say hello? How about sending "one flower" to the desk of every woman that works for you or a chocolate bar to every guy? Hell, they could trade between them if they wanted to. Do this JUST BECAUSE!!! LOYALTY IS VERY INEXPENSIVE....... Coddling will suck you dry.

Humanity.......

Can you even "summarize" humanity? Hold my beer, I'm going to try.

After forty-eight years of life, I have seen humanity dive like it is in the Olympics. Twist, turn, and flip with no splash upon entry.

"WE ARE SUPPOSED TO ADVANCE AS HUMANS, YET ALL WE HAVE DONE IS DISSOLVE HUMANITY"

Parents, you chose life, and thank you for doing so, but then you throw it away by letting others raise your gift. You say you do not have time but if you really look at it...you do not "make" time. Your kids are begging for attention from you. If they don't get it from you, they will find it in a stranger. Just like kids that turn into gang bangers. They do not have a family, so they turn to the only thing that they think is a family. Unfortunately, this does not usually turn out well for them. Tell your kids you love them. Show them that you want to listen to them, but DO NOT coddle them.

BE THE PARENT…. not the friend. You are supposed to prepare them for the world and yet it is amazing how many fail miserably at this simple task. Let them see you lead by example. We have thrown away two generations that absolutely might be the laziest walks of life ever on earth. Do not let there be a third. You still have time to change some of them and your grandchildren.

Tell your kids to put the phones down. Have family dinners together. Take a road trip and make them look out the windows and see this unbelievably gorgeous thing we live on called EARTH.

ENJOY FREEDOM and all it stands for. Please stop thinking the government can take care of you. STUDY ECONOMICS and you will see the true answer. NOT ONE COMPANY the government has ever put together has been profitable. NOT ONE!!!!! (EXAMPLE….POST OFFICE AND VA HOSPITAL, SOCIAL SECURITY, CALIFORNIA, WASHINGTON STATE, OREGON, NEW MEXICO, NEW YORK, DC, ETC) Teach your kids what it took to be free because their teachers are not. Teach them about the World Wars, Lewis and Clark, Landing on the Moon and the fall of the Berlin Wall. The school system sucks so if you do not teach them…they will not be taught correctly. They are only taught to take tests. The so-called "educators" have sold their souls to the dollar as well as the unions and it is one big agenda now….PROVE ME

WRONG!!!!! A fifth-grader of yesteryear could out read, outwrite and spell better than most high school graduates of today. Makes you proud huh?

Question your government....IT IS YOUR RIGHT AND YOUR RESPONSIBILITY!!!! No matter what side you lean toward if something isn't inherently right for HUMANITY everyone should speak up. IF YOU DON'T LIKE LIVING IN A FREE COUNTRY...MOVE!!!! Don't fuck up something that is so good when you have a world of shit you can move to. DO YOU GET IT YET?

Like I said before, "We keep eating the fruits of Freedom, but we have stopped watering the tree." When that tree is gone, it will not grow back. There are so many amazing people in this world that need us to fight for freedom in hopes that one day, they, and their children may experience it.

Most of all, BE HUMAN. It isn't all about you. You are going to leave a legacy of your existence whether you want to or not. How are people going to remember you? It's your choice, and you only get one try at it. Make it count.

AUTHOR'S NOTE

WELL, YOU MADE IT THROUGH. SOME OF YOU
are cursing me and going to leave a bad review, while some
of you love what I wrote and are looking for a sequel.
Then there are those in the middle that are like "that was
entertaining," and you will go on with your everyday life.
For the price of a fast-food meal, worst case, I got some
kind of emotion out of you.

Please note that although I use a good bit of profanity
in this book, it is to make a point. I am a very passionate
person and maybe one of the most giving people of my
time with what I have to offer. You don't know me. Some
of you never will. But, know this......I care for humans
and most of all for the humanity we pass to the next generations. I don't care what color, sex, religion, or sexual
orientation you are. I just want HUMANITY to open its
eyes and see facts. Stop letting the media mold your amazing brain. Stop letting your political choice put you in a
tunnel vision of how the world operates. There are those

in this world that are very evil. They want to manipulate your thought process to gain as much power as they can. YOU CONTROL EVERY ASPECT OF LIFE......KNOW THIS!!!!

We have an amazing world. WE HAVE AN AMAAAAAAAAAAAAAAAZING WORLD!!! If we could figure this out................ we can do great things. If we keep letting the powers that be divide us without looking at FACTS................ we are doomed.

God Bless all that came before us that built and fought for this great Nation. I said "great," not perfect. Tell your mom and dad we said hey and God Bless you and your family. God Bless our Freedom we have, and God Bless America. The last beacon of Freedom on earth.

Dahc Slokin

GLOSSARY

FUCK SHIT....... something so messed up it deserves two cuss words

Assclown.........an individual that is so delusionally STUPID they don't deserve any other name

Bless your heart...........southern way of saying "fuck off" hidden in niceness

Snowflake........... generation of kids that thinks they know it all and had parents that coddled them their whole life while being groomed at socialist schools.

Common Sense............the ability to know how to function in life without being told.

"In the weeds" ....widely used in the restaurant industry meaning you are getting your ass handed to you and you can't get food out fast enough.

Hypochristians.........those that verbalize about following God but their actions prove them liars.

Trojan Horse…………look it up…it's history you were probably not taught.

Sheep………………..those that follow aimlessly not able to think for themselves

Puking up a Shit Sandwich………. Spewed stupidity that only a fucktard would say not realizing how it hurts their business.

Fucktard………… one that is so insanely stupid that truth and facts escape them.

Dillholes……… IDIOTS!!!

Hold my Beer………….. Southern for "if you think that is good, ya'll need to watch this shit!!!

FREEDOM….The greatest gift given to humanity.